Building on a Dream

# The International Space Station

Tamra B. Orr

Purple Toad Publishing

PURPLE TOAD PUBLISHING



Printing 1 2 3 4 5 6 7 8 9

BUILDING ON A DREAM

Big Ben
The Burj Khalifa
The Eiffel Tower
The Empire State Building
Fallingwater
The Flatiron Building
The Golden Gate Bridge
The Great Wall of China
The International Space Station
The Leaning Tower of Pisa
The Louvre
The Space Needle
The Statue of Liberty
The Sydney Opera House
The Taj Mahal
The Trevi Fountain
The White House

**Library of Congress Cataloging-in-Publication Data**
Orr, Tamra, B.
Building on a Dream: The International Space Station / Written by Tamara B. Orr.
p. cm.
Includes bibliographic references, glossary and index.
ISBN 9781624694370
1. The International Space Station — Juvenile Literature. 2.—Space Stations—Juvenile Literature. 3. International Cooperation—Juvenile Literature. I. Series: Building on a Dream: The International Space Station
TL797 .B55 A45 2019
629.44/2

**Library of Congress Control Number:** 2018944208

**eBook ISBN:** 9781624694363

**ABOUT THE AUTHOR:** Tamra B. Orr is a full-time author in the Pacific Northwest. She has written more than 500 educational books for readers of all ages. A graduate of Ball State University in Muncie, Indiana, Orr and her family enjoy camping whenever the weather cooperates. Since arriving in Oregon, she has had the chance to see some amazing celestial events, including the solar eclipse of 2017. She keeps an eye on the sky so she can spot the International Space Station as it flies over.

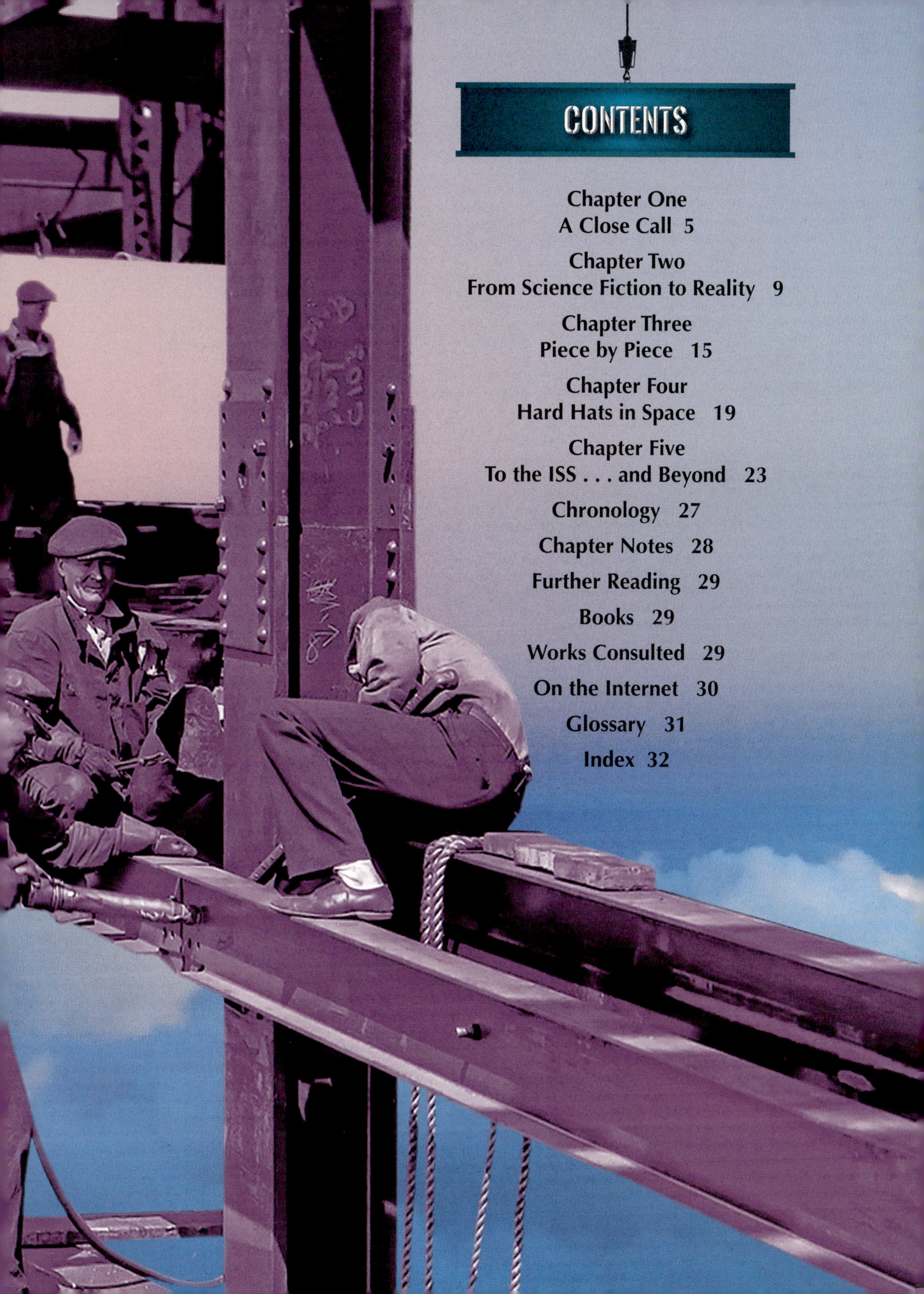

# CONTENTS

(Top) A weather satellite orbits Earth. More than 500,000 pieces of space debris orbit the planet. Along with man-made debris, there are countless meteoroid particles. Most of this space junk is too tiny to see. Some is the size of a marble. About 20,000 pieces orbiting Earth are larger than a softball. "The greatest risk to space missions comes from non-trackable debris," said Nicholas Johnson, NASA's chief scientist for orbital debris.[1]

CHAPTER 1

# A Close Call

The crew aboard the International Space Station (ISS) in July 2015 knew about the dangers of space debris. This debris, or "space junk," zips through the blackness at speeds of up to 17,500 miles per hour. (That is ten times the speed of a bullet on Earth.) Debris the size of a paint fleck can crack glass when it is going that fast. In the past, NASA had always notified the ISS crew hours ahead of time that debris was heading for them. The astronauts would then fire special jets built into the ISS. These jets allowed them to move the space station out of the way to safety.

It didn't happen quite like that this time. A fragment of a Russian weather satellite appeared on NASA's monitors at 6:30 a.m. It was moving at eight miles per second. It looked as if it would strike the ISS in just 90 minutes.

American astronaut Scott Kelly and Russian cosmonauts Mikhail Kornienko and Gennady Padalka were told to shut the ISS down and evacuate immediately. They rushed to seal off each of the station's modules in case one of them was hit. Then the crew scrambled to the *Soyuz*. This Russian capsule is typically used to take astronauts to and from the space station. The capsule also functions as an escape pod in an emergency. In the 15-year history of the ISS, this was only the fourth time astronauts had ever had to use the capsule for safety.

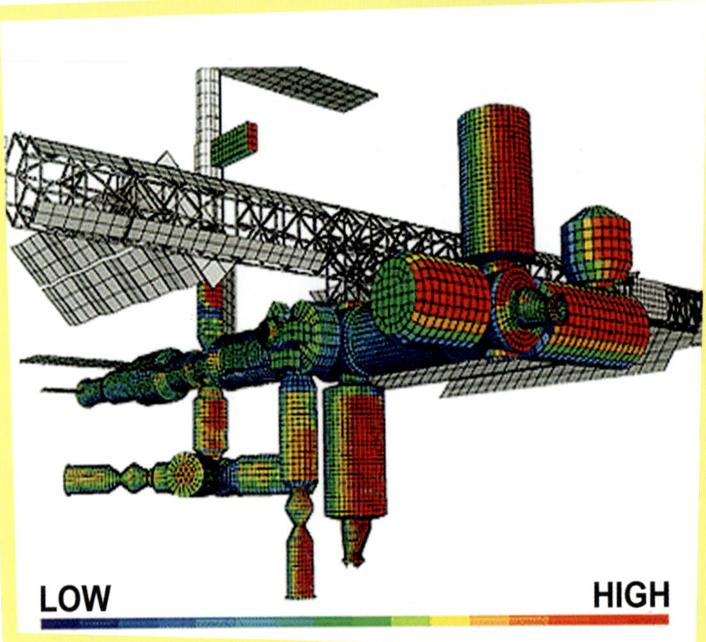


On the ISS, the areas shown in red are at the highest risk of impact from space debris.

At 8:01 a.m., the satellite debris sped by without any contact with the ISS. NASA gave the anxious crew an "all clear" seconds later. Astronaut Kelly tweeted, "Happy there was no impact. Great coordination with international ground teams. Excellent training." It was a close call, but everyone, and the ISS, was safe.[2]

**Scott Kelly takes a selfie inside the *Cupola*.**

The International Space Station is considered one of the most amazing structures human beings have ever built. It is easy to understand why. The ISS took seven types of vehicles, ten years, 16 countries, 136 shuttle flights, 1,000 spacewalk hours, and more than $100 billion to build. It remains the most expensive and complex structure in history.

**The completed ISS is 357 feet long and weighs 925,335 pounds. More than 8 miles of electrical wire connects its thousands of solar cells to electrical devices on board. These include 52 computers, which operate using about 2.3 million lines of code. Astronauts Alexander Gerst and Serena Auñón-Chancellor work with the computers inside the *Destiny* lab.**

(Above) The Soviet Union postage stamp, which celebrates Cosmonautics Day, features Konstantin Tsiolkovsky. (Right) One of Tsiolkovsky's first spaceship designs was a sphere.

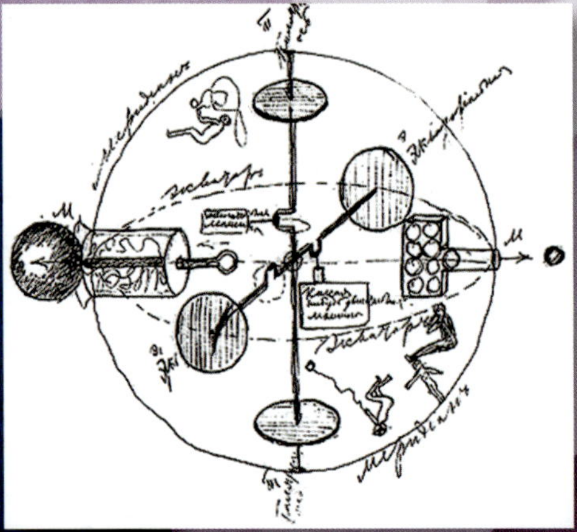

CHAPTER 2

# From Science Fiction to Reality

Do you know who first came up with the idea for a futuristic place where people could live in space? If you guessed a NASA scientist or a computer engineer, it would make sense. But you would be wrong. The first people to imagine a space station were mainly science fiction authors.

In ancient Greece, Aristophanes wrote a play about a paradise in the sky called Cloudcuckooland. Gulliver traveled to the flying island of Laputa in 1726's *Gulliver's Travels*. In 1869, Edward Everett Hale wrote *The Brick Moon* for the *Atlantic Monthly*. It included a sphere shot into space with people aboard.

In 1920, Russian teacher and rocket scientist Konstantin Tsiolkovsky drew a blueprint for a space station in his book *Beyond the Planet Earth*. The station had a greenhouse, laboratory, living quarters, and docking area. Its six crewmembers were all from different countries. A few years later, rocket engineer Hermann Oberth coined the term *space station*.

Most space stations in science fiction stories were described as circular. They rotated to simulate Earth's gravity. Some were small, with just enough room for the crew. Others were imagined as big as a city. However, these ideas remained a fantasy.

After World War II, attitudes about space travel began to change. In 1952, *Collier's* magazine printed scientific articles about space exploration. The authors, including German rocket scientist Wernher von Braun, mentioned the need for a space station.

***Sputnik 1* was barely the size of a beach ball.**

In 1957, Russia placed the satellite *Sputnik 1* in low Earth orbit. As Newton's first law of motion states, an object in motion will stay in motion unless something pushes or pulls on it. With little friction in low Earth orbit to slow it down, an object will keep moving in one direction. Gravity pulls it toward Earth just enough to keep it circling the planet.

In 1958, the U.S. government founded NASA, the National Aeronautics and Space Administration. One of its first goals was to build a workable space station. Before much could be done, however, Russia surprised the world again. On April 12, 1961, Soviet pilot Yuri Gagarin became the first person to fly into space.

U.S. President John F. Kennedy feared that America would fall behind Russia in technology. In May, he asked Congress to fund a project that would land a man on the moon. "Now it is time to take longer strides . . . ," he stated, "time for this nation to take a clearly leading role in space achievement, which in many ways may hold the key to our future on earth."[1] NASA's focus turned from building a space station to flying astronauts to the moon.

**Yuri Gagarin**

The push was successful. In February 1962, American John Glenn orbited

John Glenn enters the *Friendship 7* capsule to make history.

Earth. Just over seven years later, on July 20, 1969, U.S. astronauts Neil Armstrong, Edwin "Buzz" Aldrin, and Michael Collins landed on the moon. When Armstrong stepped out to walk on the moon's surface, he uttered what would become one of the most familiar quotes in history: "That's one small step for man, one giant leap for mankind."

In May 1973, the U.S. placed Skylab in orbit. This short-term space station was used to train astronauts to be in space for long periods of time. From Skylab, engineers learned about what astronauts do and do not need in space. The showers and toilets on the ISS were part of these necessities.

In addition, Skylab helped scientists improve communications. As Skylab orbited Earth, radio signals would be interrupted. To solve this, a fleet of eight

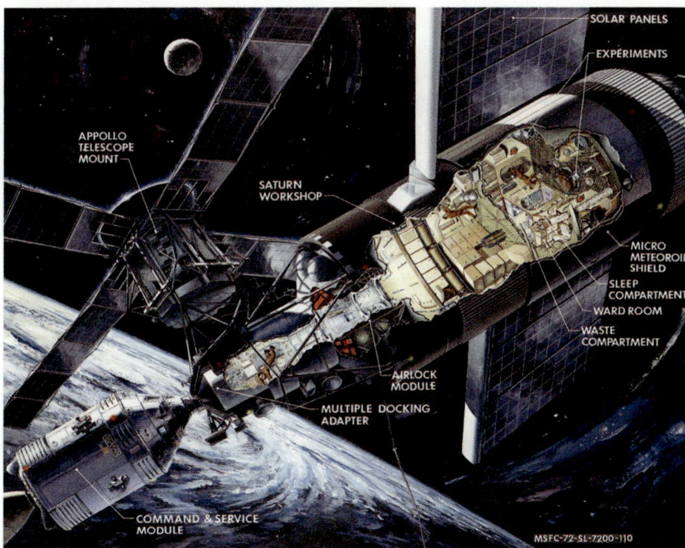


**From experiments on Skylab (above), scientists learned how to preserve water. Nearly 94 percent of water expelled from the ISS crew is reused.**

aircraft equipped with special antennas relayed the signals from the space station to Houston. Later, satellites in fixed orbits over the equator would replace the aircraft.

After a year, Skylab was abandoned. It orbited in space until it reentered Earth's atmosphere in July 1979. As it was spiraling toward its eventual disintegration over Australia, the Russians were setting new records. In 1971, they launched Salyut 1. This space station orbited Earth almost 3,000 times over 175 days. For three of those weeks, it had a crew of three. By 1979, six crews had gone up to Salyut, carried by Soyez rockets. They not only set endurance records (96 and 140 days), but they welcomed space travelers from other countries, including Poland, Czechoslovakia, and Germany.

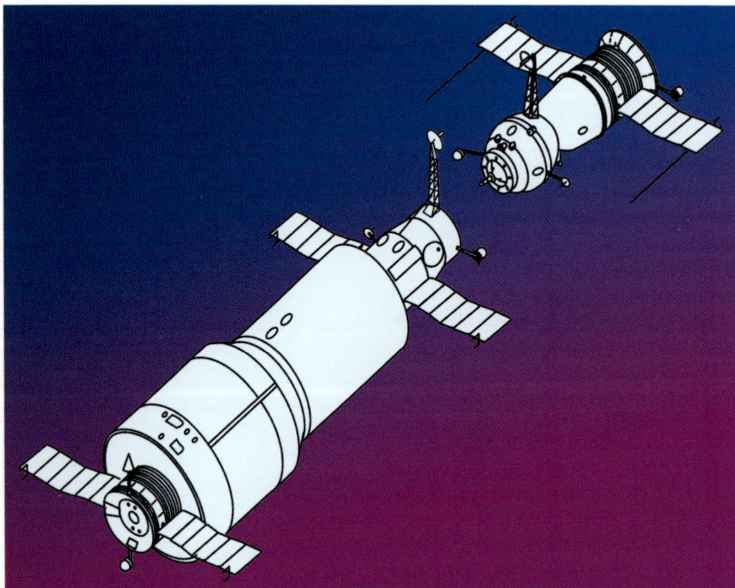

**The Salyut 1 and *Soyuz* (right) prepare to dock. Visible at the rear (left) of Salyut 1 is a propulsion module. Both craft are powered by Soyuz-type solar arrays.**

The United States again stepped up to meet Russia's challenge. On April 12, 1981, the U.S. launched the space shuttle *Columbia*. Shuttles were designed to repeatedly go to space and then come back and land like an airplane. *Columbia* orbited Earth 37 times and successfully landed again.

**Space shuttle *Challenger***

In January 1984, U.S. President Ronald Reagan renewed the country's commitment to the ISS. "Our progress in space, taking giant steps for all mankind, is tribute to American teamwork and excellence . . . ," he stated. "America has always been greatest when we dared to be great. We can reach for greatness again. We can follow our dreams to distant stars, living and working in space for peaceful, economic, and scientific gain. Tonight, I am directing NASA to develop a permanently manned space station and to do it within a decade."[2]

Then tragedy struck. On January 28, 1986, space shuttle *Challenger* lifted off from Kennedy Space Center in Cape Canaveral, Florida. On board were six astronauts and a high school teacher. A mere 73 seconds after liftoff, the shuttle became a ball of smoke and fire. The entire crew was killed.

**Teacher-in-Space Christa McAuliffe (left) with *Challenger* crew Gregory Jarvis, Judith Resnik, Dick Scobee, Ronald McNair, Mike J. Smith, and Ellison Onizuka**

Just one month later, on February 20, Russia's space station Mir was launched. Described by some as "a 100-ton Tinker Toy," Mir was the oddest, largest structure the world had ever seen in outer space.[3]

(Left) U.S. President George H.W. Bush, with Neil Armstrong at his side, announces plans to build Space Station Freedom (above, artist's idea).

CHAPTER 3

# Piece by Piece

After the shuttle disaster, virtually all space development was halted, including the designs for the International Space Station. Instead, experts focused on what went wrong on the shuttle to make sure it did not happen again.

On July 20, 1989, President George H.W. Bush addressed a crowd at the National Air and Space Museum. He said, "In 1961 it took a crisis—the space race—to speed things up. Today we don't have a crisis; we have an opportunity. To seize this opportunity, I'm not proposing a 10-year plan like Apollo; I'm proposing a long-range, continuing commitment. First, for the coming decade, for the 1990s: Space Station Freedom, our critical next step in all our space endeavors. And next, for the new century: Back to the Moon; back to the future. And this time, back to stay."[1]

Space Station Freedom was designed and redesigned over the next several years. Funding came and went. Eventually experts realized that to make this dream a reality, space agencies from around the world would need to work together. Five agencies contributed their time, money, materials, and skills. Sixteen countries were involved: the United States, Russia, Canada, Japan, Belgium, Brazil, Denmark, France, Germany, Italy, the Netherlands, Norway, Spain, Sweden, Switzerland, and the United Kingdom. The ISS became the largest international program in world history.

The ISS is huge—far bigger than most people imagine. Finished, it would be the size of a football field. It would weigh almost one million pounds. The solar panels alone would spread over an acre. The living quarters were designed to be the size of a six-bedroom home, with two bathrooms and a gym. Building the ISS on the ground and then launching it into space would be impossible. There was no engine in the world powerful enough to do it.

Instead, the ISS would have to be built in space. Piece by piece, it was taken into orbit, 240 miles above Earth's surface. Then, it was assembled. The project was slow, expensive, and incredibly challenging.

In November 1998, the first module was launched. The Russian-built *Zarya* (meaning "dawn" or "sunrise") lifted off from the Baikonur Cosmodrome in Kazakhstan. This module helped provide battery power, fuel storage, and a docking station for the next module.

The second was launched in early December from the United States. The *Unity* module rode up on NASA's space shuttle *Endeavour.* Every few months, another shuttle would take up more supplies and materials for the astronauts building the ISS. The huge solar array was sent up in 2000, with more panels added in 2002. In 2008, both the European Space Agency's Columbus Laboratory and Japan's Kibo Laboratory were added to the ISS.

**A space shuttle carries the *Leonardo* module to the ISS in 2001.**

The men and women constructing the ISS were working in one of the most difficult environments possible. The ISS moves at five miles per second, so it orbits Earth 15.5 times a day. The astronauts' environment varies from frigid cold and dark to blazingly hot and bright every 92 minutes. John Shannon, NASA's launch flight controller in 1998, told *All About Space*, "We've learned a lot since that first module. I think the really tough part to me of learning how to build this enormous structure in space was that it had to be a viable spacecraft the whole time. It wasn't just like a ship you can build in dry dock and launch when it's all finished up. We had to really think through how all the systems would work as we were building it out in the most hazardous environment that people can operate in."[2]

In late 2000, the ISS's first crew came to stay. Astronaut Bill Shepherd was joined by cosmonauts Yuri Gidzenko and Sergei Krikalev. They stayed for several months, helping to set up the station's interior and, as Krikalev stated in an interview with NASA, "making it come to life."[3] The ISS had become a reality.

**Yuri P. Gidzenko, William M. Shepherd, and Sergei K. Krikalev were the first crew to live on the ISS.**

And then the unthinkable happened again. In February 2003, space shuttle *Columbia* was carrying a group of scientists from the space station back to Earth. It exploded, killing all seven people on board. Once more, work on the space station paused as people thought of the universe as more frightening than fascinating.

Spacewalking astronauts assemble the ISS as it passes over New Zealand. They use drills and other tools (top) to install exterior cameras.

CHAPTER 4

# Hard Hats in Space

Imagine watching a house being built. First the foundation is made, then the walls, the interior support, and finally the roof. Can you see the hammers and saws? The piles of lumber and buckets of nails?

Now try to imagine building something in space, dealing with light and dark, extreme temperatures, bulky space suits, and no gravity. The people who built the ISS had a daunting challenge—but also an amazing adventure. Progress on the ISS had been on hold, but at last, it was time to move forward again.

Astronaut Kent Rominger told PBS, "Building the space station is not an ordinary construction job." He pointed out how hostile and isolated space can be. One of the biggest obstacles was that every step had to be figured out before it was actually started. "If you're building a house and you cut a two-by-four to a certain length and you go to install it and it doesn't work . . . you toss that board, you go cut another one, and you're off and running," he explained. "If we show up in space, and now that piece that we're putting on doesn't fit, we're out of luck. That may have just delayed the next series of missions."[1]

Julie Payette, a Canadian astronaut, pointed out that not only do you have to have the right materials, but you also have to have the right tools. "As I often say to people, unfortunately, there is no hardware store around the corner, so if you forgot a particular type of washer or you don't have the right screwdriver, well, you can't go back and get it."[2]

**Oleg Kononenko and Anton Shkaplerov use telescoping booms. These look like fishing rods and are used to move massive components outside the station.**

Putting together the ISS used many of the same skills as the ones used to construct aircraft on Earth. It also relied heavily on what was learned from the earlier construction of Mir. Cables had to be attached, screws needed to be turned, and pieces needed to be carefully fit together. One of the biggest challenges in space is that, like in a swimming pool, if you push or turn something in one direction, your body goes the opposite way. The reaction is far worse in space. Astronaut Jim Newman told PBS, "So if you have an electric drill . . . and loosen a bolt, and you're not tied down with your feet or your hands, you can feel it trying to turn you the other way."[3] Staying tethered to the ISS is essential. The tether is made of wire on a spring-loaded spool. It is attached to the ship and to the astronaut. That way, if an astronaut slips or stumbles, the tether can pull him or her back in. Astronaut Mike Gernhardt adds, "If you didn't have the tether and you let go, even if you're two inches away from the station, you can't swim over there."[4]

On top of coping with all of these conditions, astronauts have to figure out how to do their jobs when encased in thick space suits. To prepare for it, they train in the Neutral Buoyancy Lab, a swimming pool where, Newman says, "you have to learn to be one with the suit."[5]

Gernhardt is an expert at spacewalking. He describes how difficult it can be to move in these outfits. "Inside the suit, you're constantly

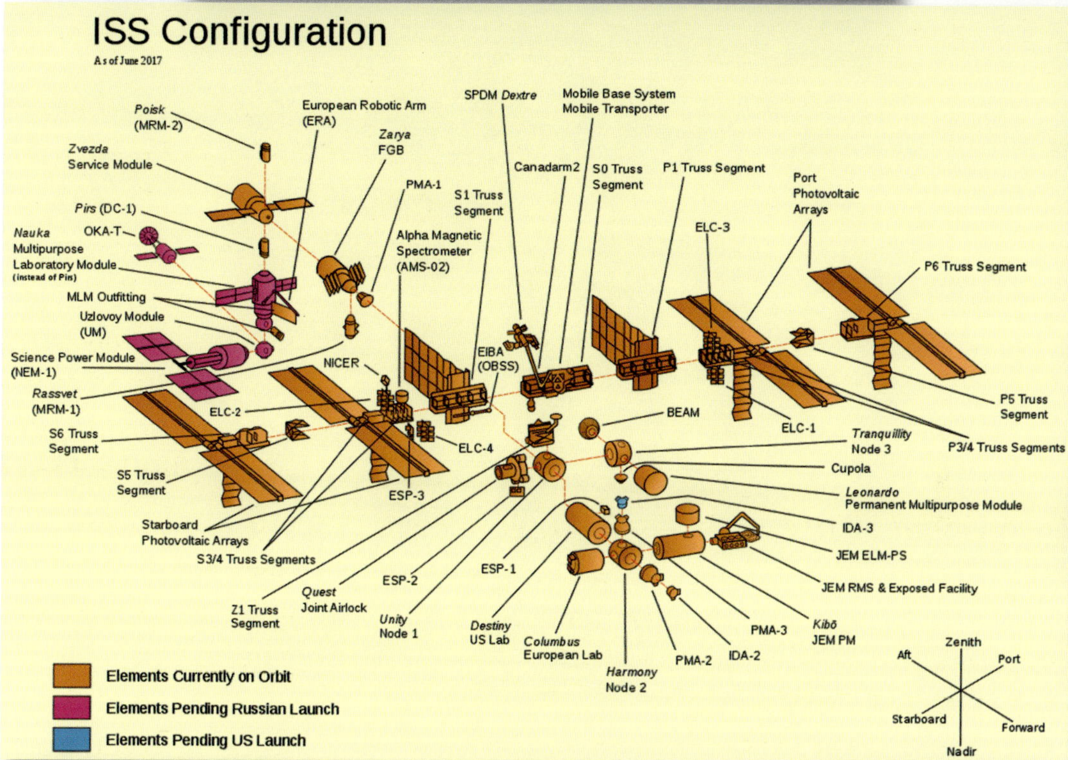


**The many components of the ISS had to be put together in space. Each of these pieces was shuttled into orbit, then attached by the space station crew.**

flexing all of your muscles to keep control," he stated to PBS. "If you start [spacewalking], and then you go to stop—you put on the brakes with your hand—you're going to pitch up. Your feet are going to tend to fly up over your head."[6]

As well designed as the suits are, they can be damaged. What happens then? Gernhardt explains that first the oxygen would leak out and the pressure would drop. If it drops too far, the astronaut will get the bends. If it drops even farther, the astronaut may not have enough oxygen to stay conscious. A backup oxygen pack is added to most suits to be used in an emergency. "A big leak—like a big hole in the suit, say a half-inch hole or something like that, or if your glove blew off—would pretty much be a real bad day for you," he added.[7]

Astronaut Robert L. Curbeam Jr. works on solar panels. They are kept facing the sun using gyroscopes. Orbital height and velocity are maintained using the thrusters of docked spacecraft.

CHAPTER 5

# To the ISS . . . and Beyond

It took a decade to finish building the ISS. When it was finally complete in 2000, it had three main modules connected by nodes. The U.S. module is *Destiny*. The European one is *Columbus*. The Japanese one is *Kibo* (Hope). In 2010, the U.S. module *Tranquility* was added.

Each module has a specific function. According to astronaut Tom Jones, who helped activate the module, *Destiny* is "the guts of the Space Station's research and command and control capabilities."[1] *Columbus* is where a great deal of experiments in life sciences, fluid physics, and material sciences take place. It has 10 phone-booth-sized racks to hold all of the experiments. *Kibo* has two research facilities in it. *Tranquility* houses much of the ISS's life support systems and a special treadmill called the C.O.L.B.E.R.T., or Combined Operational Load-Bearing External Resistance Treadmill. (It was named in honor of late-night talk-show host Stephen Colbert.)

Besides the modules and all their laboratories, another amazing feature is the Canadian-made 55-foot-long robot arm, the Canadarm2. (The first Canadarm rides to and from Earth on shuttles.) The arm is incredibly strong and, according to astronaut Rominger, it "can literally walk from one end to the other. The beauty of this is that, as the station grows and becomes very large, you'd have a hard time designing any arm to do everything you wanted it to do . . . either end of the arm can attach itself to any point on the station. So ideally you attach to an area where you need to work, and if a week later or days later you need to work in another area of the station, you can walk the arm around the station to position it to a more usable space to work."[2]

**Dextre sits above the *Destiny* lab. Its "hands" are power tools.**

When the ISS needs external batteries changed or cameras replaced, it is not always an astronaut who has to do it. The crew can also ask Dextre, the handyman robot from Canada. Dextre can hitch a ride on the Canadarm2 to get between worksites. The robot stands 12 feet tall and weighs 3,664 pounds. U.S. and Canadian teams both operate Dextre from the ground.

The space station has three main purposes. First, it does research to help improve life on Earth. Thousands of experiments are done to further medical research and develop new materials. Second, it helps scientists get a better idea of what life in space is like and how it affects people. John Shannon, NASA's former launch flight controller, told *All About Space*, "[On the ISS] we've seen physiological changes in bones and eyes, pressure on your spinal cord, and a lot of different things that we never would have known if we were just doing two-week flights on the Shuttle. . . . the ISS is this wonderful safe test bed where you can

NASA astronaut Kjell Lindgren captures a floating shipment of fruit for the crew of the ISS.

experiment on crews so that when we do go beyond low Earth orbit we can do so much more safely." He concluded, "I think that's going to be the legacy of the ISS."[3] Third, the ISS provides a place for other spacecraft to dock. It has had visitors from Russia, Japan, and Europe and from Elon Musk's company, SpaceX.

How long will the ISS last? Approximately $3 billion a year is spent to maintain and update it. Originally experts believed the satellite would be in orbit only until 2016, but former U.S. President Barack Obama extended that until at least 2024.

Eventually the ISS, as high-tech as it is, will begin to wear out. What happens next? Like the Mir space station, the ISS is too big to remain in orbit. Vitaly Davydov, deputy head of the Russian space agency Roscosmos, told *All About Space*, "After the ISS completes its mission, we'll have to sink it. It can't be left in orbit because it's too complex and heavy. It could produce a lot of junk."[4] One plan is to guide the station back to Earth and let it break up over the ocean. Another plan is to reuse at least one module to build a new space station.

# Chapter 5

**The ISS has been so successful, plans for future space stations and missions are already in place.**

How will NASA follow up after the ISS? By 2015, they had already started working on that. "We, the government, want another viable space station before this one ends," stated Sam Scimemi, ISS director at NASA. He told *Space News*, "If the space station ends in the 2020s and there's nothing to follow it, we will have lost all of this effort in research and benefits to humanity."[5] Scimemi and many others believe that the next space station will be built by a private company rather than by governments.

However, an official statement signed on September 27, 2017, between NASA and other space agencies may change that. The statement commits these groups to working together to build a space station near the moon. Referred to as a "deep space gateway," this station would provide a place for astronauts to test new systems needed for journeys into deep space.[6]

While no one is sure what type of structure will be built in space next, they all know one thing. Someone will build it—and it will be a big challenge and an even bigger adventure.

# Chronology

| | |
|---|---|
| **1923** | The term *space station* is used for the first time. |
| **1952** | Wernher von Braun and other scientists write about creating a space station. |
| **1957** | Russia places *Sputnik 1* into orbit. |
| **1958** | The U.S. government forms NASA. |
| **1961** | Yuri Gagarin becomes the first human in outer space. U.S. President John F. Kennedy challenges the country to reach the moon. |
| **1969** | U.S. astronauts land on the moon. |
| **1969–1972** | Five more manned missions reach the moon. |
| **1973** | Skylab is put into space. |
| **1975** | U.S. Apollo spacecraft and Russian Soyuz spacecraft successfully dock and undock in space. |
| **1979** | The abandoned Skylab reenters Earth's atmosphere and breaks apart; pieces land across Western Australia; Salyut astronauts set records for endurance in space. |
| **1981** | The first space shuttle flies into space and returns to land safely on Earth. |
| **1984** | U.S. President Ronald Reagan calls for the International Space Station (ISS) in his State of the Union Address. |
| **1986** | Space shuttle *Challenger* explodes shortly after liftoff. Russia places the first piece of its space station, Mir, into orbit. It paves the way for the ISS. |
| **1989** | U.S. President George H.W. Bush requests more space exploration. |
| **1998** | The first module of the ISS is launched. |
| **2000** | The first crew comes to stay on the ISS. |
| **2001** | Mission control guides the abandoned Mir space station back to Earth. Pieces of it land in the South Pacific. Canadarm2 is added to the ISS. |
| **2003** | Space shuttle *Columbia* explodes after entering Earth's atmosphere. |
| **2005** | The U.S. lab module is added to the ISS. |
| **2008** | The European lab module and the Japanese lab module are added to the ISS. |
| **2010** | The U.S. module *Tranquility* is attached to the ISS. |
| **2015** | Space debris comes very close to hitting the ISS. |
| **2017** | NASA, Roscosmos, and other ISS partners plan to build a space station near the moon. |
| **2024** | The ISS is scheduled to be decommissioned. |

**Chapter 1**

1. NASA. "Space Debris and Human Spacecraft." NASA, September 26, 2013.
2. Woods, Jonathan. "Space Junk Forces Space Station Crew to Seek Shelter." *Time*, July 16, 2015.

**Chapter 2**

1. Kennedy, John F. "May 25, 1961: JFK's Moon Shot Speech to Congress." Space.com, May 25, 2011.
2. Reagan, President Ronald. "State of the Union Address, 25 January 1984." NASA.gov.
3. Zak, Anatoly. "How Mir Became Humanity's Foothold in Space." *Popular Mechanics*, February 19, 2016.

**Chapter 3**

1. Lydon, Christopher. "Presidential Space Speeches." Radio Open Source, February 16, 2007.
2. O'Callaghan, Jonathan. "15 Years of the ISS: The Past, Present, and Future of the Space Station." *All About Space*. November 20, 2013.
3. "2010 Interview: Sergei Krikalev." NASA, International Space Station, October 27, 2010.

**Chapter 4**

1. PBS. "Astronauts in Hard Hats." PBS, November 2000.
2. Ibid.
3. Ibid.
4. Ibid.
5. Ibid.
6. Ibid.
7. Ibid.

**Chapter 5**

1. "Destiny Laboratory." NASA, March 8, 2010.
2. PBS. "Astronauts in Hard Hats." PBS, November 2000.
3. O'Callaghan, Jonathan. "What Will Happen When the ISS Is Decommissioned?" *All About Space*, December 29, 2012.
4. Ibid.
5. Foust, Jeff. "NASA Urged to Develop Post-International Space Station Strategy." *Science News*, March 9, 2015.
6. "NASA, Roscosmos Sign Joint Statement on Researching, Exploring Deep Space." NASA Press Release, September 27, 2017.

# Further Reading


**Books**

Hamilton, John. *International Space Stations: The Science Lab in Space*. Minneapolis: A&D Xtreme, 2017.

Hearst, Michael. *Curious Constructions*. San Francisco: Chronicle Books, 2017.

Hogan, Christa. *Space Stations*. Burnsville, MN: Focus Readers, 2018.

Kissock, Heather. *The International Space Station*. New York: Weigl, 2017.

Larson, Kirsten. *International Space Station*. Vero Beach, FL: Rourke Educational Media, 2017.

Morey, Allan. *International Space Station*. Minnetonka, MN: Bellwether Media, 2017.

**Works Consulted**

Foust, Jeff. "NASA Urged to Develop Post-International Space Station Strategy." *Science News*, March 9, 2015. http://spacenews.com/nasa-urged-to-develop-post-international-space-station-strategy/

Kennedy, John F. "May 25, 1961: JFK's Moon Shot Speech to Congress." *Space.com*, May 25, 2011. https://www.space.com/11772-president-kennedy-historic-speech-moon-space.html

Klose, Kevin. "2 Cosmonauts Break Record for Endurance," *Washington Post*, July 15, 1979.

Lydon, Christopher. "Presidential Space Speeches." Radio Open Source, February 16, 2007. http://radioopensource.org/presidential-space-speeches/

"Mir Space Station." NASA History. https://history.nasa.gov/SP-4225/mir/mir.htm

"NASA, Roscosmos Sign Joint Statement on Researching, Exploring Deep Space." NASA Press Release, September 27, 2017. https://www.nasa.gov/feature/nasa-roscosmos-sign-joint-statement-on-researching-exploring-deep-space

NASA: International Space Station. https://www.nasa.gov/mission_pages/station/main/index.html

O'Callaghan, Jonathan. "15 Years of the ISS: The Past, Present, and Future of the Space Station." *All About Space*, November 20, 2013. https://www.spaceanswers.com/space-exploration/15-years-of-the-iss-the-past-present-and-future-of-the-space-station/

O'Callaghan, Jonathan. "What Will Happen When the ISS Is Decommissioned?" *All About Space*, December 29, 2012. https://www.spaceanswers.com/space-exploration/what-will-happen-when-the-iss-is-decommissioned/

Palmer, Katie. "ISS Crew Prepares to Evacuate in Real-Life 'Gravity' Scare." *Wired*, July 16, 2015. https://www.wired.com/2015/07/iss-crew-prepares-evacuate-real-life-gravity-scare/

PBS. "Astronauts in Hard Hats." PBS. November 2000. http://www.pbs.org/wgbh/nova/station/hardhats.html

Reagan, President Ronald. "State of the Union Address, 25 January 1984." NASA.gov. https://history.nasa.gov/reagan84.htm

"Salyut Crew Hailed for Record in Space," *New York Times*, March 5, 1978. http://www.nytimes.com/1978/03/05/archives/salyut-crew-hailed-for-record-in-space-americans-send.html

Wilford, John Noble. "Salyut May Yield Permanent Space Station." *New York Times*, April 17, 1979. http://www.nytimes.com/1979/04/17/archives/salyut-may-yield-permanent-space-station-salyut-may-yield-permanent.html

Woods, Jonathan. "Space Junk Forces Space Station Crew to Seek Shelter." *Time*, July 16, 2015. http://time.com/3961500/international-space-station-debris/

Zak, Anatoly. "How Mir Became Humanity's Foothold in Space." *Popular Mechanics*, February 19, 2016. http://www.popularmechanics.com/space/a19517/mir-space-station-30th-anniversary/

**On the Internet**

To subscribe to this app and know when the ISS will be going overhead, check out NASA's Spot the Station at
https://spotthestation.nasa.gov/

To watch what the ISS crew is doing—or what the planet looks like when they are sleeping—go to NASA's live stream at
http://www.ustream.tv/channel/live-iss-stream

For a look at each part of the ISS and what it does, go to PBS's program "Stationed in the Stars" at
http://www.pbs.org/wgbh/nova/station/blueprintleft.html

Watch a documentary on the construction of the ISS at https://www.youtube.com/watch?v=R_xmf-v6VZc

Watch a brief time lapse of the construction of the ISS at https://www.youtube.com/watch?v=Kie53ZDcSYE

Listen to and watch a TEDTalk about the ISS at
http://thekidshouldseethis.com/post/how-the-international-space-station-was-built-ted-ed

**aeronautics** (air-oh-NAH-tiks)—The science of flight.

**bends**—A painful condition caused when a change in pressure causes bubbles to form in the blood.

**cosmonaut** (KOZ-muh-not)—A Russian astronaut.

**decommission** (dee-kuh-MIH-shun)—To take out of service.

**evacuate** (ee-VAH-kyoo-ayt)—To immediately leave a place; to empty out quickly.

**gyroscope** (JY-roh-skohp)—A wheel that is mounted to spin freely around an axis and can turn in any direction.

**malfunction** (mal-FUNK-shun)—To fail to work normally.

**meteoroid** (MEE-tee-or-oyd)—A mass of rock in space.

**module** (MOD-jul)—A self-contained unit that can be combined with others and easily rearranged.

**node** (NOHD)—Another term for module.

**orbital velocity** (OR-bih-tul veh-LOS-ih-tee)—The minimum speed that will keep a satellite or other body in orbit.

**physiological** (fih-zee-uh-LAH-jih-kul)—Relating to how the body works.

**satellite** (SAT-eh-lyt)—An object that orbits another, larger object.

**simulate** (SIM-yoo-layt)—To imitate.

**spacewalk**—To work in space, outside the spacecraft.

**thruster** (THRUS-ter)—A small rocket engine on a spacecraft used to adjust its flight path.

**PHOTO CREDITS:** Cover, pp. 6, 7, 11, 13, 14, 16, 17, 18, 20, 21, 22, 23, 24, 25—NASA; Back cover, p. 1—Creative Commons; p. 4—State Farm; pp. 4, 8, 9, 10, 11, 12—Public Domain; p. 13—Acroterio. Every measure has been taken to find all copyright holders of material used in this book. In the event any mistakes or omissions have happened within, attempts to correct them will be made in future editions of the book.

# Index